Overcoming Fear of Abandonment

The Ultimate Guide to Overcoming Fear of Abandonment and Getting Rid of Abandonment Issues for Good

by Wilson Ferguson

Table of Contents

Introduction 1

Chapter 1: Building Healthier Relationships 7

Chapter 2: Getting Back to Where It All Began 11

Chapter 3: Finding Yourself and Becoming Self-Sufficient 17

Chapter 4: Practicing Acceptance 23

Chapter 5: Forgiving and Forgetting the Past 27

Conclusion 31

Introduction

Of the most prevalent fears around the world, is the fear of being alone. We have all evolved into social beings, and our very existence depends on our numbers. These fears usually stem from childhood, where a person might have experienced a traumatizing effect - such as the loss of a parent or friend through moving away, divorce, death, or lack of physical or emotional care. The abandoned person grows up and has huge trust issues in their own adult relationships, usually stemming from the feeling that someone they are close with, whether it's a friend, spouse, fiancé, girlfriend/boyfriend, or even a family member, will desert them in the future. Then, in order to prevent this from happening, he or she engages in unhealthy behavior that actually ends up hurting the relationship more than helping it, thus making the abandonment more and more likely.

Do you see how this is a pattern of self-destruction, that can lead you closer to the exact thing you're most afraid of? The pattern is unintentional though. And partially even subconscious.

The fear of abandonment from traumatic childhood experiences doesn't even have to stem from a parent or loved one actually abandoning them. It can also occur as a result of a parent ridiculing them, and/or emotionally abusing them, or neglecting them. There are those who first develop a significant fear of abandonment in adulthood as well, typically through a traumatic loss of a loved one through a bad break-up, divorce, or death.

People who suffer from this fear sometimes choose to go to a therapist. The therapist would examine the person's background, and attempt to discover which traumatic event(s) may have caused this fear, determining whether it started in childhood or adulthood. Over time, the therapist would teach the patient how to separate the fears of the past from the present, so they can begin the healing process by developing the ability to lessen the grip that the fears have on them.

Although therapy is often effective, it certainly is not the only thing that a person with abandonment fears can do to help themselves. You may be able to overcome these abandonment issues on your own – through a little effort – and finally be able to build flourishing relationships once again, without panicking about what may or may not happen in the future. This book is designed to help you do exactly that, so let's get started!

© Copyright 2014 by LCPublifish LLC - All rights reserved.

This document is geared towards providing reliable information in regards to the topic and issue covered. The publication is sold with the idea that the publisher is not required to render accounting, officially permitted, or otherwise, qualified services. If advice is necessary, legal or professional, a practiced individual in the profession should be ordered.

- From a Declaration of Principles which was accepted and approved equally by a Committee of the American Bar Association and a Committee of Publishers and Associations.

In no way is it legal to reproduce, duplicate, or transmit any part of this document in either electronic means or in printed format. Recording of this publication is strictly prohibited and any storage of this document is not allowed unless with written permission from the publisher. All rights reserved.

The information provided herein is stated to be truthful and consistent, in that any liability, in terms of inattention or otherwise, by any usage or abuse of any policies, processes, or directions contained within is solely and completely the responsibility of the recipient reader. Under no circumstances will any legal responsibility or blame be held against the publisher for any reparation, damages, or monetary loss due to the information herein, either directly or indirectly.

Respective authors own all copyrights not held by the publisher.

The information herein is offered for informational purposes solely, and is universal as so. The presentation of the information is without contract or any type of guarantee assurance.

The trademarks that are used are without any consent, and the publication of the trademark is without permission or backing by the trademark owner. All trademarks and brands within this book are for clarifying purposes only and are the owned by the owners themselves, not affiliated with this document.

Chapter 1: Building Healthier Relationships

The biggest thing that kills any kind of relationship is the lack of communication. Or, to be more specific, the lack of *good* communication. If you know that you have a fear and have no idea where it is coming from, you should be willing to open up and talk to your partner about it. Don't see it as just your problem: if you are in a relationship with someone, the problem belongs to both of you. If you have an idea of where it may have originated, talk to him or her about it. Express your desire to overcome it, and change, and that you need their help to achieve that. Don't ever make them think that it is their job to do this for you, though. Their responsibility is only to help through being supportive and understanding where you are coming from. The change itself must come from within you.

The first step in getting rid of the fear of abandonment is to build a life for yourself that isn't entirely entrenched in another person. Do not be so engrossed in the relationship that you give the power to your partner to keep you safe. That's just setting yourself up for disaster. If that person leaves, you are definitely going to feel alone, and maybe even take desperate measures because you made yourself so vulnerable to them. You need to perceive yourself as an individual first, before you can have a healthy partnership.

Ensure that you understand your self-esteem issues, and don't let them get in the way. Try to eliminate any parent-child behavior that may exist between you and your partner. If you depend wholly on your partner for emotional support, take steps to correct that. For example, you should know on your own whether or not you look attractive today, regardless of whether or not your partner complimented you this morning. And if you recently achieved something fantastic, you should be able to feel great about it, even if your partner hasn't yet acknowledged it.

Finally, work towards building trust in your relationship. Trust is built in the everyday interactions we have with the people around us. If there is no emotional interaction, then you cannot build trust with that person. Don't force a person to share with you emotionally, or understand your emotional needs. Trust usually develops over time, through a back and forth of give and take. I tell you a small secret. You tell me a small secret. I make a confession about my feelings. Then you make a confession about yours. Each exchange of these intimate details and feelings gets you deeper and deeper into a relationship of trust. What you might be surprised by though, is how you may be the one holding back for fear that your step might not be reciprocated. My best advice here is to start small, but also start first. Don't wait for your partner to guide you into a level of deep trust, because you never know, your partner may be waiting for your guidance as well. Somebody has to go first, and it might as well be you.

If you and your partner both want to build a stronger emotional relationship, then the underlying assumptions and fears that either party holds must be identified, openly communicated to one another, and then faced and challenged. From a selfish perspective, your feelings may seem a higher priority than your partner's, but you must also make sure that your partner's feelings are secure as well. It doesn't work as a one-way street. When you and your partner tend to each other's emotional needs, a strong trust between you will be formed and your fears of abandonment will be reduced.

Chapter 2: Getting Back to Where It All Began

Just like any other fear, the key in getting rid of this fear is to confront it directly.

You need to dig deep, and try to figure out exactly when and how this all started. With most of us, the fear of abandonment and other fears started in our childhood, the most vulnerable time of our lives. So think back to your earliest memories, and try to pinpoint what may have caused it. Did your parents work a lot, leaving you on your own? Did your old brother join the military and you never knew if or when he'd be coming home? Did you get lost at the zoo during a class field trip and think you'd never find your way back? It could be anything, and it may even be multiple things. Start brainstorming and see what you come up with.

Children are very susceptible human beings, absorbing everything that happens before them in their environment. They have limited experience of the world, and take on everything that is taught to them or happens to them. They have malleable minds like playdough, and the simplest of events can change behaviors in an instance. This is why fears are mostly started in childhood - the adult brain is more developed with its own belief systems, and therefore less susceptible to taking on new fears.

One of the reasons that these fears surface in us sometimes, is the influence our parents had on our development. Not every case of a fear of abandonment is from the parent actually leaving the home. A child can feel neglected and alone, while their parents are right there sitting next to them. These fears often stem from emotional non-support, or else bad communication that occurs between the child and the parent. The parent will either ignore the child when they need interaction most, or discourage the child from coming to them because they are so unapproachable. Basic things like threatening and scolding a child can cause fear and resentment. Most of these issues are simply miscommunications between the parent and the child, wherein the child doesn't understand what he or she has done wrong, and the parent does not understand what exactly the child needs.

Actual abandonment by a parent – when one parent does actually leave the home – tends to have a more significant impact on a child. But then again, in homes where the remaining parent stayed and took wonderful emotional care of the child, he or she may have ended up perfectly fine. But in a lot of cases, being 'abandoned' by even one parent causes great emotional and psychological distress, especially when he or she was close to that parent. The child will feel betrayed, and oftentimes will wonder what they did wrong to make their parent leave. If you've ever thought these things, it's time now to fully comprehend the fact that you did nothing wrong, and sometimes these things just happen. If you had had a parent that raised you alone, be grateful for that one parent. If you didn't have any, be thankful for the person that raised you as their own as well. Gratitude is a powerful tool that can help you to accept what happened in your past in a different, more positive light.

Then, sadly, there are those whose parents died. Death is a very traumatizing event for anyone, especially for children. Do not suppress the memories. Instead, understand what happened, and remember all the great memories you had while they were still here with you. Of course, you will still feel heartbroken from the absence, but you will feel a whole lot better if you keep the good memories close to your heart, and allow the bad ones to fade away.

The majority of our fears develop during our childhood years, but a lot of our fears also develop during our adult years as well. One would think that because we are wiser as adults, we should be able to handle our fears better. However, we often partake in habits and behaviors that, unknowingly, can make those fears even worse. One of the fears in our adult stage that we develop is the fear of rejection. We all want a mate, and in doing so, we go about talking to those of the opposite sex that we like, in the hopes of starting a relationship with them. But at one point or another, we will all experience the feeling of rejection. It is not a nice feeling, and when it happens, our self-esteem can take a nose-dive to an all-time low as we ask ourselves a thousand questions about what went wrong. This fear of rejection then feeds into our fear of abandonment, as we fear that the person we do ultimately end up having a relationship with will also eventually reject us and leave.

One needs to understand that when someone rejects us that does not always mean that something is inherently wrong with us. This is important, and embracing this truth will save you a lot of pain. Think about all the times you were rejected. Then smile, and understand that there was nothing wrong with you. Not everyone will always like you, just as you will not always like everyone. And that's OK. Think about it this way: If everybody likes everybody, then any two people could be in a relationship, which would make being in a relationship pretty mundane and insignificant. What makes a partnership so special is the fact that it can't just be with anybody.

Finally, our fears often stem from us not knowing the future, or even our uncertainty of the present. It seems to be human nature to fear the unknown, and we create objects, legends, stories, and myths in our minds to try and explain them. This lack of knowledge has a tendency to cause intense emotional turmoil. But should we seek to gain knowledge on these unknowns? Should we visit crystal ball fortune tellers or palm readers? No. The beauty of life is such that you simply don't need to know certain things. However, it doesn't hurt to ask your partner about anything that you want to know. If your partner believes you should know, then you will be told. But don't force the issue, and don't let it grow into a bigger problem in your mind.

Whether our fears developed in our childhood, or our adulthood, much of the problem can be fixed by embracing one simple concept: Acceptance. But more on that later…

Chapter 3: Finding Yourself and Becoming Self-Sufficient

Children cannot take care of themselves, and therefore will need a caretaker for their basic needs. Out of all the primates and mammals, humans actually depend upon this care and nurture of others for a longer period of time. But going into adulthood, our dependency can be more of a curse than a blessing. The reason why a lot of us fear abandonment is because dependency is hard-wired into our brains for survival. As we talked about earlier, we have all experienced this fear at one time or another in our lives, so managing this fear can be difficult. But one thing we can do to cut the emotional umbilical cord for good is find ourselves.

Become Self-Sufficient.

As we get older and move out of our parents' homes, self-sufficiency is something that has to be learned in order to survive. But we don't ever become *totally* self-sufficient, do we? We need to be dependent in some way or another, but if that dependency overshadows other qualities that can cause problems. So how can you find yourself to become more self-sufficient? The enlightening journey discussed in this chapter will help you to do exactly that, and therefore become less emotionally dependent on others, and more emotionally independent. Doesn't that sound great?

The first thing to do is to become fully conscious and aware of yourself. It sounds complicated, but it's really not. In order to understand who you are, and what you can become, you need to start distinguishing your thoughts from others'. Understand how your mind works, what your preferences and tastes are, and what makes you the way you are. For a moment, be introspective, without any concern for anybody else. Look into your belief system and understand why you believe the things you do. Is it because your parents, family, or friends told you to believe them? Is it because society tells you they're true, and that if you don't, then you are a pariah or a misfit? One of the things wrong with our society today is that we idolize conformity, and crucify those who are different. Never be afraid of who you are, and never be afraid to show who you are to the person you're in a relationship with. When people experience this fear, they often change who they are to "please" their partner so that they won't leave. You have to be upfront with your partner from the get-go, instead of waiting down the line to show a side of yourself that could be new to them, and risk scaring them off.

Next, start relying on yourself. This way, you'll start building up self-confidence, even if you don't realize it. Don't be swayed by what people say all the time. Think for yourself, and create your own set of values, and take necessary action on your own. Often, people with low self-esteem will think their opinion is not as valid as others around them, and they often are afraid to express themselves. You have to be more assertive when it comes to the things you know and believe, and ***start trusting in your own judgment and decision-making***.

Give yourself more "you" time. This will help you to immerse yourself into your own thoughts and emotions, and give you a better understanding of who you are. At first you probably won't like it, and you may even feel anxious, wanting to call friends, or be around your partner. Likely, you'll feel stuck, thinking about what they may be doing without you. Let me assure you though, these feelings are only temporary, and once you start spending time alone regularly, you'll come to treasure that time, and feel unhappy if you don't get enough of it. Solitude is important, and it will help you gain independence, which will lessen your fears of abandonment. If you are happy with yourself, you will not fear being alone. And if you're not happy with yourself, then this will be a great time to change that. Find things that you like doing by yourself. This could include reading, cycling, surfing the internet, watching videos of cute dogs on YouTube, etc. Do more of these things by yourself, and kick the urge to involve your partner. Just don't become a hermit, obviously. Space out your solitude time, for example two-three hours every other day.

Abandon all your negative thoughts, and replace them with positive ones. It's pretty simple. Just make a mental effort to nourish positive thoughts, minimize judgmental attitudes of yourself and others, and open your mind to new possibilities. If you catch yourself thinking of something negative, then say to yourself "okay that's a negative thought. Let me think about this positive thing instead" and then come up with something (anything!) that's positive, and allow your mind to ponder it.

Chapter 4: Practicing Acceptance

Acceptance is a key factor in all of this. Everyone has fears in some form or another. We all feel vulnerable at times, we all feel afraid to lose someone we love at times, and we also feel emotionally distraught at times. As human beings, we have to face each of these obstacles in order to grow. Don't look at these fears and emotions as stumbling blocks - but as stepping stones to reach the emotional state that you need to be in.

When we accept a romantic partner into our life, these are the things that we sign up for. It will not all be roses and chocolate. There will be times when you are happy, but there will also be times when you are sad, and there will also be times when you are extremely angry with each other. When these things happen, don't see it as bad. View these events with a more positive outlook. Because we are all different, and have our different opinions and views of the world, they will clash at one time or another. When this happens, this should be seen as an opportunity to grow your bond stronger, rather than tear it apart. This is what should happen in your other relationships also, such as with your friends. Don't fear fights, and instantly think that a breakup will happen because of it. Your bond will always bring you closer together, and it would take a very powerful force to break that bond.

Not only must you accept the differences in your relationships, you must also accept yourself. Accept your fears. Everyone has at some point or another experienced the fear of being abandoned, while some may experience it more strongly than others. We also have to accept the origins of our fears. We can do so by finding solutions, letting go, and finding the beauty in everything that is occurring.

When negative things occur, don't complain. This goes for the things that happened in the past as well. Stop complaining about all the bad things that happened in the past that caused you to be the way you are. It is quite meaningless to complain. By complaining, not only will you drain yourself of energy, but you will drain the energy of everyone around you. The brain often tricks you into thinking you feel better when you complain, but in reality, you actually feel worse. Use the time and energy that you use to complain more wisely. It's like a leaking roof. You can complain all you want, but if you don't go up there and fix it, then it will continue to leak every time it rains. Use your energy to identify and correct the problems that you have or had. Then take the next step in letting it go.

By letting go of certain things, you have accepted that certain aspects of life are out of your control, and that you simply have to do your very best. Life is definitely out of our control, so we can either moan about it for the rest of our lives, or face it with a smile. Accept the way life is, and bit by bit, life will look much more beautiful. There is a lot of beauty in the world. You don't have to go looking for it. Be positive, and you will start to wonder why you were ever afraid in the first place.

Chapter 5: Forgiving and Forgetting the Past

The final step in abandoning your fears is probably the hardest thing to do for any human being. Forgiveness is something we want from others, yet we find it so difficult to give it ourselves. And what could be harder than forgiving someone who probably doesn't deserve it? But for our mental state of mind and our health, we must. Your refusing to forgive the past is fueling your fears of abandonment right now, and if you don't forgive and forget the person(s) or the traumatic event, then you will forever live in the past, which affects your present as well as destroys your future.

To forgive someone, you must first understand that the hate and resentment you are giving someone is not in any way harming them. Actually, it is only harming you. Nelson Mandela once said that resentment is like drinking poison and waiting for it to kill your enemy. If you really want revenge against your enemies, or the person that hurt you in the past, live a happy and successful life. Be focused, and ensure that your current relationships don't end up like the ones in the past. Live life as if the events in the past never happened.

When you think of all the traumatizing experiences in the past that made you feel lonely, think of what it made you become, instead of how it made you feel. If you think about the person you have become, you will focus more on the positive and less on the negative. Be kind to yourself, and don't blame yourself for anything that has happened. A lot of the time, when things go wrong, we blame ourselves. This shouldn't be the case. Be kind and patient with yourself, and give yourself time to heal. You should also be open to the healing process, as your fears can sometimes cause you to lock up emotionally.

One of the most important steps you can do in forgiving and forgetting your past is to learn to *trust in the future*. You have to remember that not all humans are untrustworthy, and you shouldn't shut yourself away from the possibility of having a great time with someone else. But at the same time, you can't be naïve. Because the reality is, not everyone will have your best interests at heart. So you need to learn how to balance your trust with your instinct and internal wisdom. Wisdom will help you identify the ways in which you can prevent yourself from getting hurt. This is not an easy step, as it is often very hard to balance your wisdom and your trust. But once you have found the balance, you will be well on your way to forming healthier relationships.

The final step in forgiving is to forget. Forgiving and forgetting is often used together, because without forgetting, we often end up not ever truly being able to forgive. Sometimes, you will have to move away from the person to actually do that, and that's fine. But it is important to put the person's actions to the back of your mind. If your parent or guardian abandoned you, sometimes it takes the unthinkable act of thinking from their perspective to understand why they may have left, and forgive them. If they somehow turn up in your adult life, ensure that you talk to them and gain their perspective. From there, you can decide whether to accept them back into your life or not. But it really is important to forgive and forget in order to overcome your fears.

Conclusion

Getting rid of your fear of abandonment is crucial. We all want to belong, and if we have these fears, they will affect us for the rest of our lives by how we relate with those around us. Many people who have these issues tend to want to fix the problem only for those around them. Wrong. Ensure that you build a community, and focus more on trusting the world at large. One person cannot solve or fit all our needs, which is why we need to ensure that we build stronger relationships with those around us. If you have only one close friend, try and turn that into a larger pack of friends. This will help you to feel more connected with those around you, and you won't have those feelings of being left out anymore.

Surround yourself with those who enjoy the things that you do. Make a list of the things you love - whether it's sports, reading, gardening, traveling, playing tennis, or listening to music - and find others who share those interests. You don't have to become best of friends, but doing this will ensure that you build a better support network. This will in turn build your self-esteem and your self-confidence. Add that to the steps discussed earlier, and you will be on your way to living a much happier life!

Finally, I'd like to thank you for purchasing this book! If you found it helpful, I'd greatly appreciate it if you'd take a moment to leave a review on Amazon. Thank you!

Made in the USA
Middletown, DE
16 January 2019